Working
Snowy Weather

by Nate George

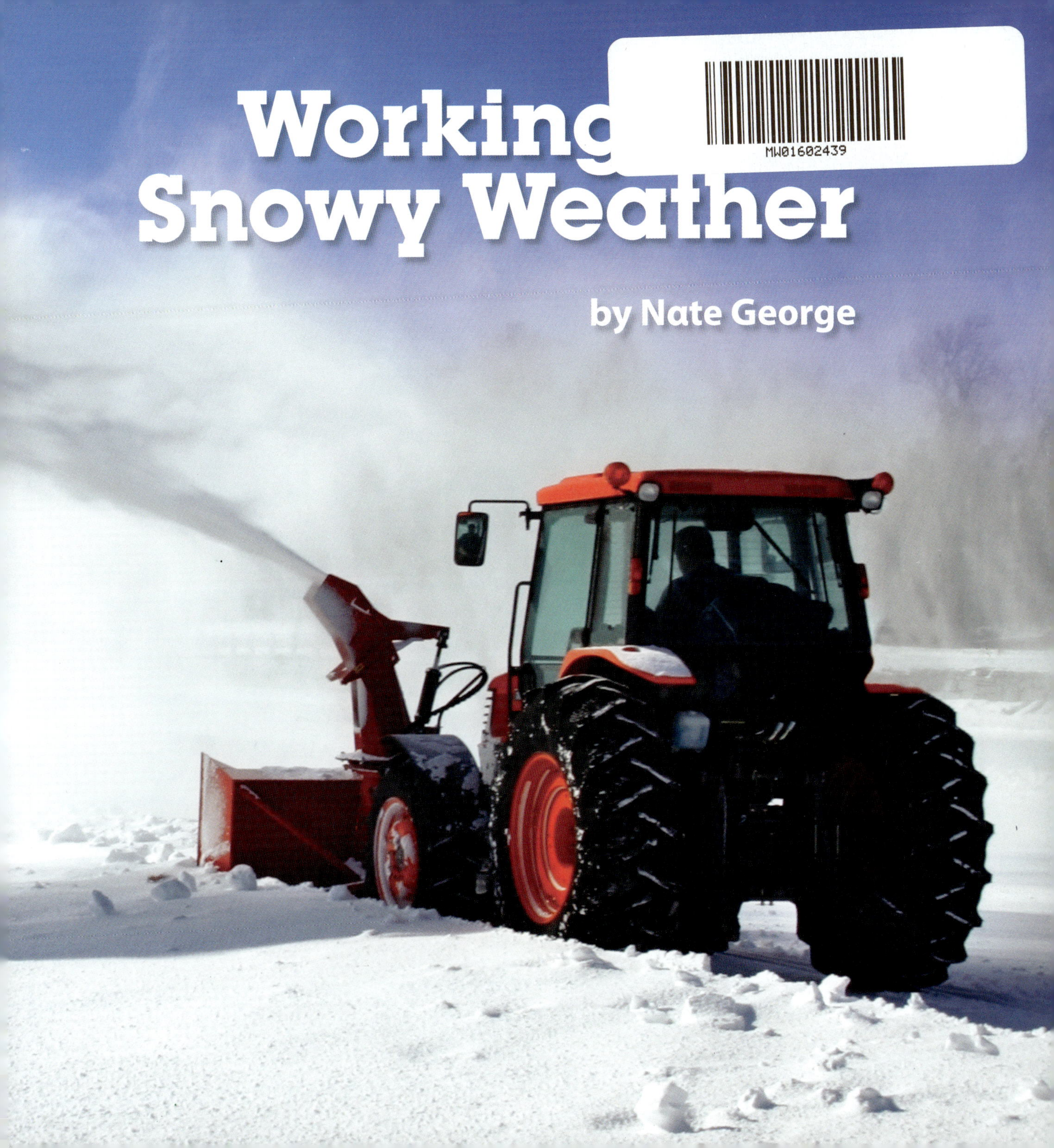

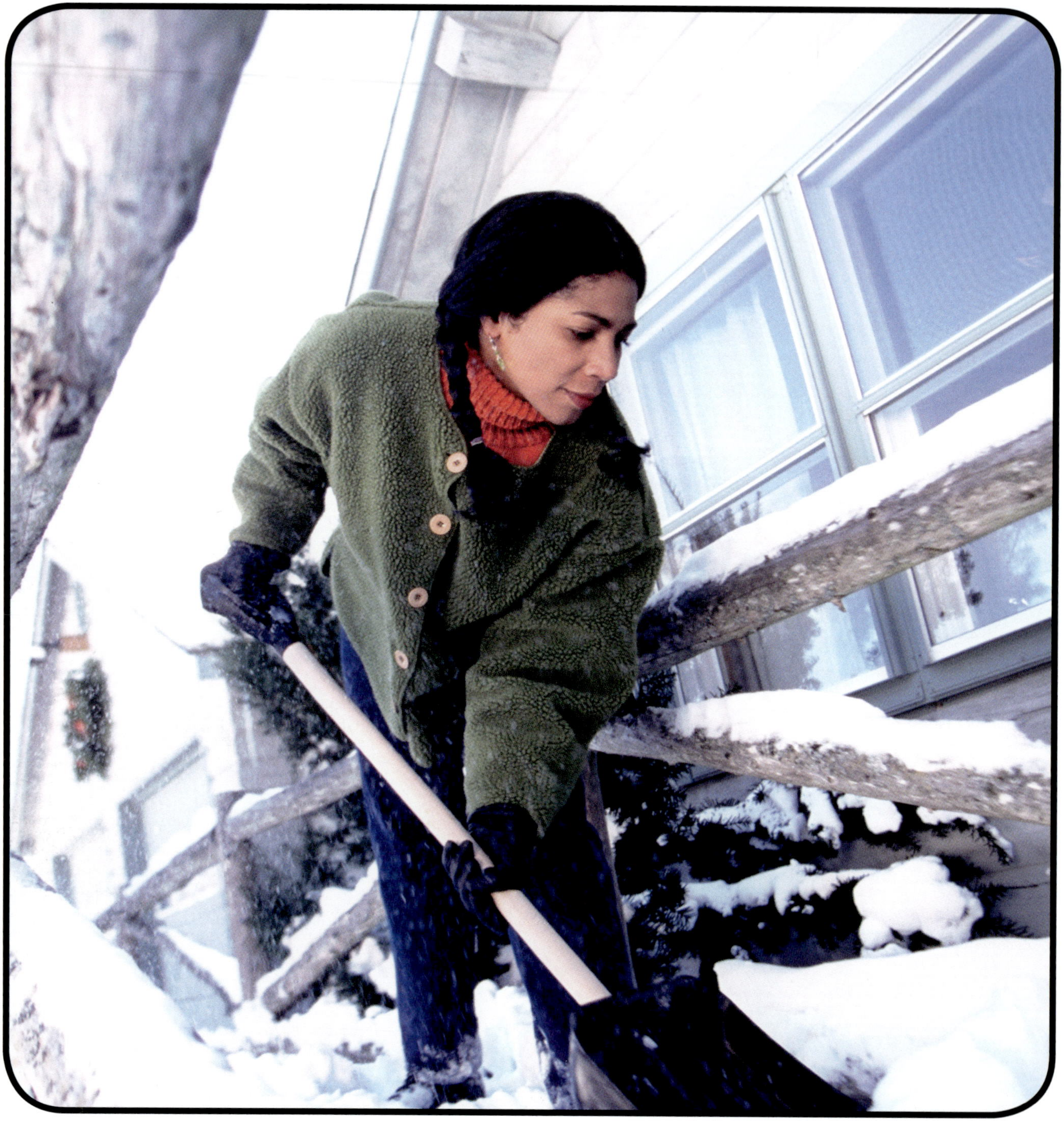

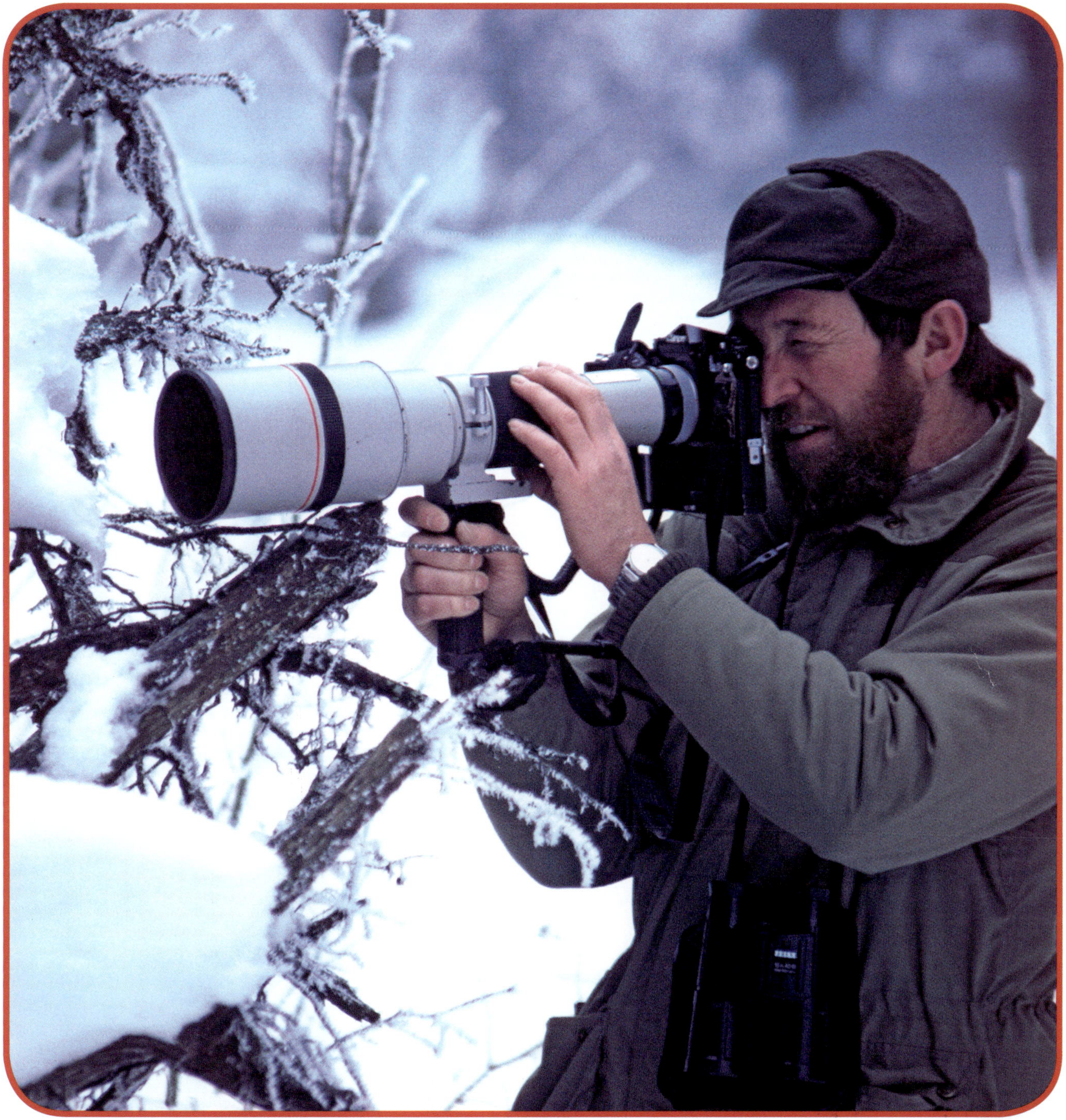

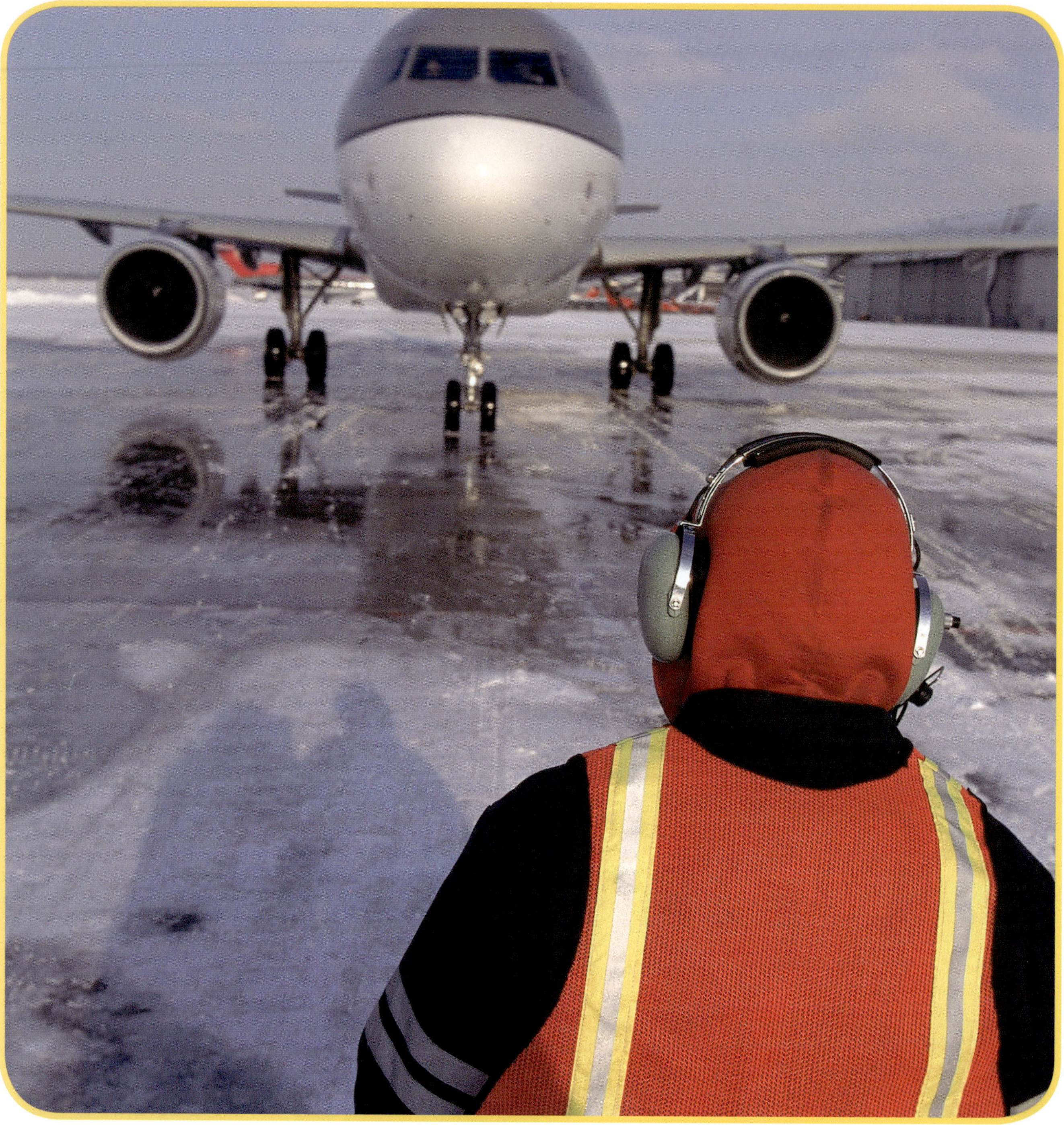

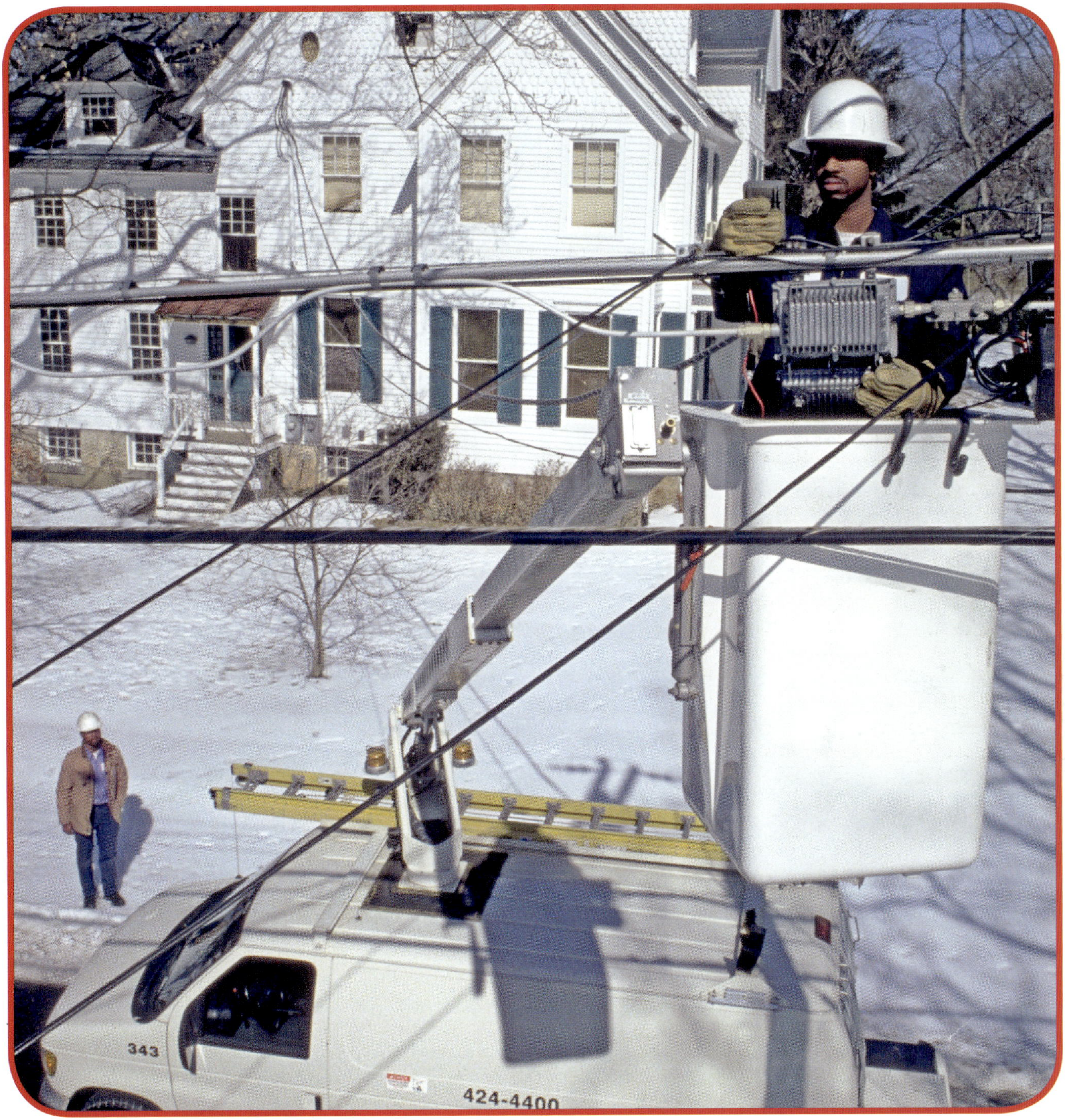
343
424-4400

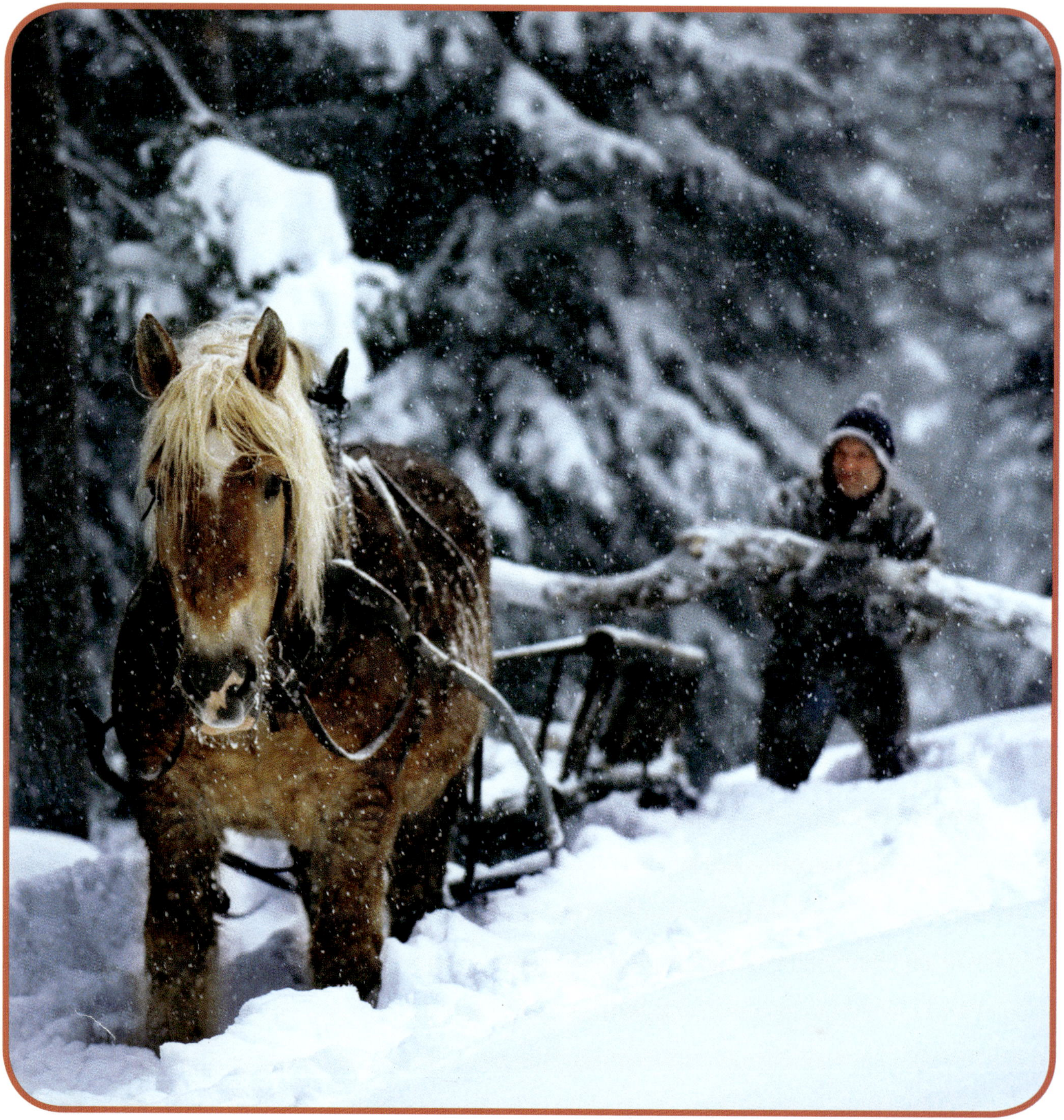

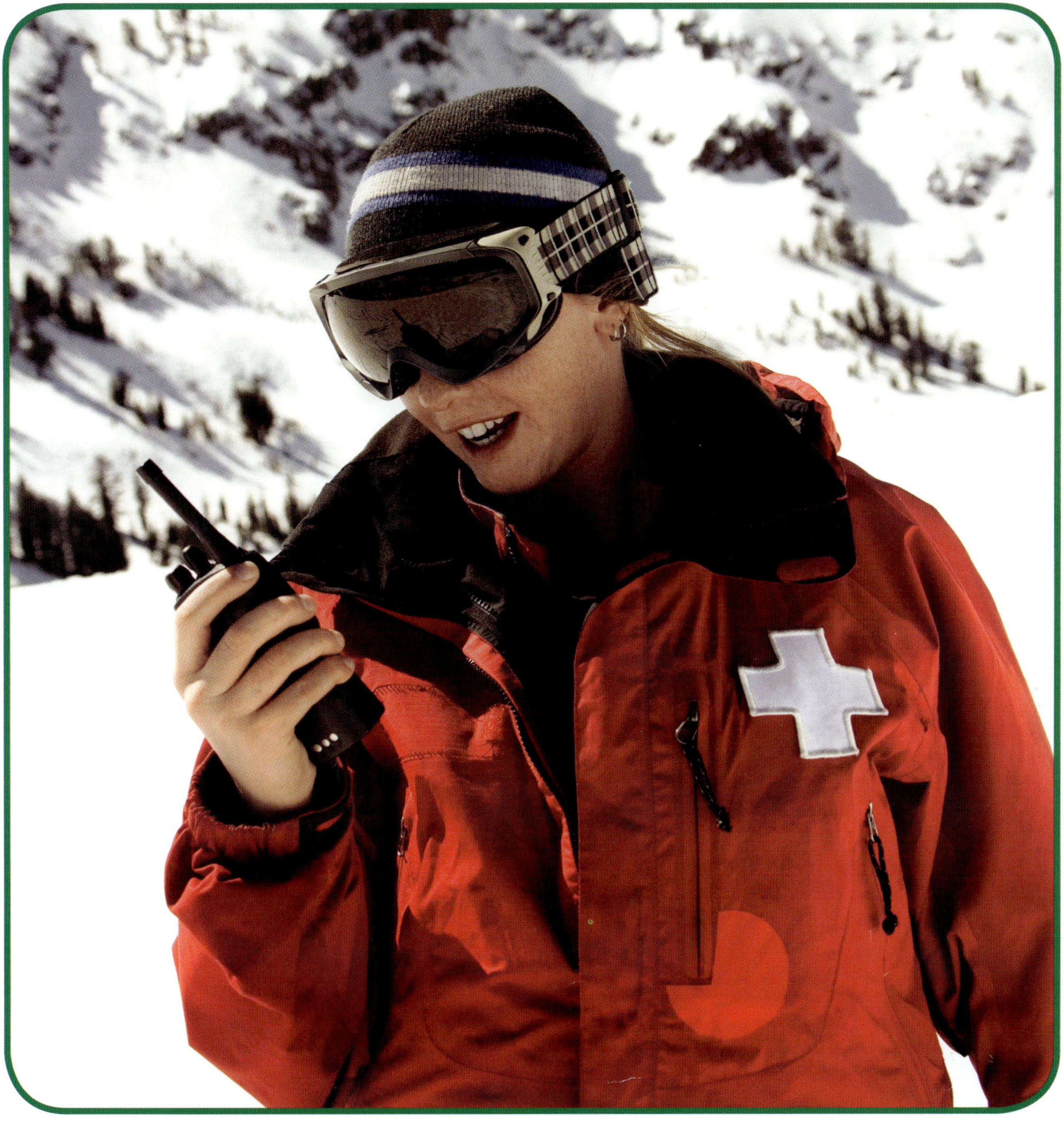

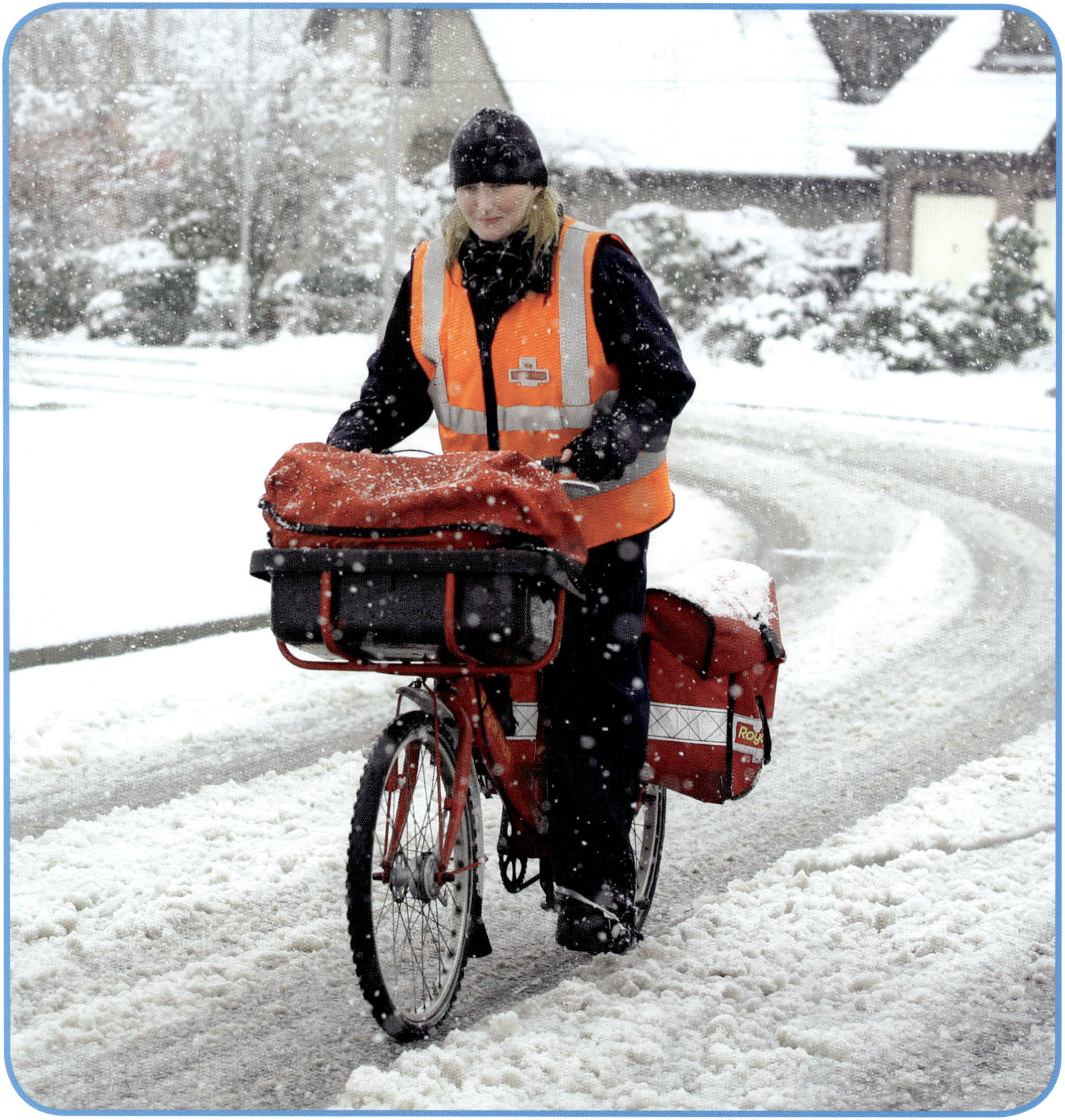